**PowerKids Readers**
*SAFARI ANIMALS*

# WARTHOGS

## Clara Reade

**PowerKiDS press**
New York

Published in 2013 by The Rosen Publishing Group, Inc.
29 East 21st Street, New York, NY 10010

Copyright © 2013 by The Rosen Publishing Group, Inc.

All rights reserved. No part of this book may be reproduced in any form without permission in writing from the publisher, except by a reviewer.

First Edition

Editor: Amelie von Zumbusch
Book Design: Greg Tucker

Photo Credits: Cover, pp. 5, 7, 9, 11, 15, 17, 19, 21, 23, 24 Shutterstock.com; p. 13 Martyn Colbeck/Oxford Scientific/Getty Images.

Library of Congress Cataloging-in-Publication Data

Reade, Clara.
 Warthogs / by Clara Reade. — 1st ed.
  p. cm. — (Powerkids readers: safari animals)
 Includes index.
 ISBN 978-1-4488-7393-7 (library binding) — ISBN 978-1-4488-7473-6 (pbk.) — ISBN 978-1-4488-7546-7 (6-pack)
 1. Warthog—Juvenile literature.  I. Title.
 QL737.U58R43 2013
 599.63'3—dc23
2011048407

Manufactured in the United States of America

CPSIA Compliance Information: Batch #CS12PK: For Further Information contact Rosen Publishing, New York, New York at 1-800-237-9932

# CONTENTS

| | |
|---|---|
| Warthogs | 4 |
| A Warthog's Life | 10 |
| Warthog Families | 20 |
| Words to Know | 24 |
| Index | 24 |
| Websites | 24 |

Warthogs have warts.

5

They live in Africa.

1

They have big teeth called **tusks**.

9

Grass is their main food.

11

They roll in mud to cool off.

13

A group of warthogs is
a **sounder**.

15

Males have four warts.

17

Females have two warts.

19

**Piglets** drink milk for five months.

21

They like to play.

23

# WORDS TO KNOW

piglets

sounder

tusks

# INDEX

**M**
mud, 12

**P**
piglets, 20, 22

**S**
sounder, 14

**T**
teeth, 8
tusks, 8

# WEBSITES

Due to the changing nature of Internet links, PowerKids Press has developed an online list of websites related to the subject of this book. This site is updated regularly. Please use this link to access the list: www.powerkidslinks.com/pkrs/wart/